MARY CASSATT

Mary Cassatt

by Jay Roudebush

CROWN PUBLISHERS, INC. - NEW YORK

Title page: SELF-PORTRAIT, c. 1880
Watercolor on paper, 13″ × 9½″ (33 × 24 cm)
National Portrait Gallery, Smithsonian Institution, Washington, D.C.

Collection published under the direction of:
MADELEINE LEDIVELEC-GLOECKNER

Library of Congress Cataloging in Publication Data
Roudebush, Jay.
　Cassatt.

　　1. Cassatt, Mary, 1844–1926.　2. Painters–United
States–Biography.　I.　Title.
ND237.C3R6813　　759.13 [B]　　78–21706
ISBN 0–517–53740–0

PRINTED IN ITALY – INDUSTRIE GRAFICHE CATTANEO S.P.A., BERGAMO – © 1979 BONFINI PRESS CORPORATION, NAEFELS, SWITZERLAND
ALL RIGHTS IN THE U.S.A. ARE RESERVED BY CROWN PUBLISHERS, INC., NEW YORK, N.Y.

LITTLE GIRL IN A BLUE ARMCHAIR, 1878. Oil on canvas, 35″ × 51″ (89 × 130 cm)
Collection: Mr. and Mrs. Paul Mellon, Upperville, Virginia

«*I am American. Simply and frankly American.*»*

A curious beginning. Why did Mary Cassatt, who had achieved so much during the course of a long and eventful career, choose those words to introduce herself to her first biographer? She was sixty-eight years old when Achille Segard called upon her in 1912, and had lived most of her adult life in France. She had received her first professional recognition from the Paris Salon, had been invited to join an art movement which was quintessentially French, and had been awarded the coveted Legion of Honor. Yet she wished to impress upon Segard — himself French — that she was American, the native of a country where she had often been slighted or simply ignored.

---

* Segard, A., *Un peintre des enfants et des mères, Mary Cassatt,* p. 2.

Perhaps Cassatt recognized American qualities in herself, qualities that did not bear transplanting despite the hospitality of the French. Certainly her hosts were often bemused at her practice of using rude peasant women and their children as models, it did not accord with their Gallic sense of elegance. And yet Cassatt, in her « simple and frank » manner, sought not elegance but strength, finding beauty in a mother's immutable love for her child rather than in some fleeting concept of style.

Cassatt was a paradoxical figure who somehow reconciled the contradictions in her life and made them work. How else does one explain a prim and proper Philadelphia spinster who was also an impassioned defender of a revolutionary art movement, a childless painter whose hallmark is maternal themes? Her sense of propriety was so acute that she once advised an agent for her good friend Henry O. Havemeyer to exercise caution in the purchase of a Titian nude, as it would be seen by Mr. Havemeyer's daughters. The same Mary Cassatt was capable of language that was nowhere nearly as delicate as her sensibilities.

She was a strong-willed individual and she came from a country built by strong-willed individuals, people who made their own rules and lived by them. In that context Mary Cassatt's opening remark to Segard makes sense.

She was born in 1844, the fourth surviving child of Mr. and Mrs. Robert Simpson Cassatt of Allegheny City (now Pittsburgh), Pennsylvania. Her father made enough money through investments to indulge his penchant for moving, and as a consequence the Cassatt household was in an almost continuous state of upheaval during her infancy.

American medicine was in only a slightly less primitive state than American culture in the 1850's, and Mr. and Mrs. Cassatt seem not to have hesitated when doctors advised them to seek a European « cure » for Robbie, the second son, who had been struck by a mysterious illness. In 1853 the family sailed for Europe and settled in Paris.

We may assume that Mrs. Cassatt, who spoke French fluently and who admired French culture, saw to it that her children accompanied her on frequent trips to the Louvre. To ten-year-old Mary it must have truly seemed a palace, filled with wonderful treasures. It is easy to imagine her pausing to watch, fascinated, as one of the many copyists who frequented the Louvre put the finishing touches to his canvas.

The Cassatts' next move led them to Germany so that the eldest son, Alexander, could continue his studies in technical engineering in Heidelberg and Darmstadt. Their sojourn was abruptly cut short by young Robbie's death, and the saddened family returned to America in 1855.

Between 1861 and 1864, Cassatt grew from adolescence to young womanhood while enrolled in the Pennsylvania Academy of Fine Arts in Philadelphia. The academy — an American model of its European counterparts — offered the prescribed classical curriculum of the day. Such a program of study would seem today to be stultifying, emphasizing as it did the endless copying of dusty plaster casts, but it appears to have suited Cassatt well enough, for it was during this period that she made up her mind to become an artist. She also decided to continue her studies in Europe, insisting — and rightly so — that she would have to cross the Atlantic if she were to properly study and learn from the old masters. America had little to offer in the form of public or private collections of art.

Robert Simpson Cassat had violently objected to his daughter's choice of a career as a painter, an unorthodox and faintly scandalous notion in that Victorian era. « I would rather see you dead, »* he told her at one point, but he eventually relented, perhaps mollified by the

---

* Segard, A., *op. cit.,* p. 5.

fact that his wife would serve as Mary's escort and see to it that their daughter was properly «set up» in Paris. Although it was not uncommon for daughters of the American *haute bourgeoisie* to attend fashionable finishing schools in Europe, they were invariably wrapped in a protective cocoon of family and friends. The Cassatts no doubt felt that they could afford to indulge Mary's whim as long as the proprieties were observed.

As an apparent concession to her anxious parents, Cassatt dutifully enrolled in the atelier of Charles Chaplin, a fashionably bland academic painter. She soon abandoned his tutelage, however, in favor of independent study at such institutions as the Louvre and the Ecole des Beaux-Arts. It was the last formal training of her career. «One does not need to follow the lessons of an instructor,» Cassatt told Segard years later, «the teaching of museums is sufficient.» *

Cassatt spent four years in Europe, and it was during this period that she made the transition from art student to professional artist. This remarkably swift change of status came about as a result of welcome news from the Paris Salon: one of her paintings, *The Mandolin Player* (1868, coll. Anthony D. Cassatt), was accepted for the Salon's annual exhibition. As Paris was the undisputed center of the Western European art world and as the Salon was the final arbiter of artistic taste, Cassatt had good reason to be proud of her accomplishment. If she thought that such recognition would vindicate her choice of a career in the eyes of her family, she was mistaken; there was a decidedly condescending note in her brother Alexander's letter to his fiancée, Lois Buchanan, when he wrote:

> «Mary is in high spirits as her picture has been accepted for the annual exhibition in Paris. You must understand that this is a great honor for a young artist and not only has it been accepted but it has been "hung on the line." ** I don't know what that means but I suppose it means it has been hung in a favorable position. Mary's art name is "Mary Stevenson" under which name I suppose she expects to become famous, poor child.» ***

Cassatt did indeed use «Mary Stevenson» as her «art name» when she signed her submissions to the Salon in the late 1860's and early 1870's. Stevenson was her middle name, and may have been used because it sounded more «American» than Cassatt.

Stylistically, *The Mandolin Player* is reminiscent of the 17th century Realists whom Cassatt greatly admired and whose work she assiduously studied. A simply dressed young Italian girl stares pensively off to the left, seemingly in the act of playing a mandolin. She is bathed in a soft light and is seated against a plain dark background. The reflective mood of this composition contrasted favorably with the mannered allegorical works which were much in vogue at the time, and probably helped to catch the attention of the members of the Salon jury.

The rapid momentum of Cassatt's career was interrupted temporarily by the outbreak of the Franco-Prussian war in 1870, which forced her to return briefly to Philadelphia. As soon as possible she braved the Atlantic crossing (ocean voyages always made her violently

---

* Segard, A., *op. cit.,* p. 8.
** To be «hung on the line» meant, as Alexander Cassatt correctly surmised, that one's work was hung at eye level, a special honor. It was customary at the time to cover the walls of the exhibition halls with paintings; works which the jury considered of lesser importance were often «skied,» or hung above eye level.
*** Quoted by John E. Bullard in *Mary Cassatt, Oils and Pastels.*

ill) and returned to Europe, this time to Parma, to study the works of Correggio and Parmigianino. It is likely that she had developed an interest in these two artists during her previous four-year stay in Europe and wished to learn more about their work firsthand. While in Parma she also learned the intaglio printmaking techniques of etching and aquatint from Carlo Raimondi, an instructor at the local academy. Though Cassatt concentrated on oil painting during the early years of her career, she would later put her training in printmaking to good use.

She was twenty-six years old when she arrived in Parma, and spoke little, if any, Italian. The citizens of Parma were accustomed to the presence of foreign artists and art historians, but the sight of this serious and hard working American *signorina* clamoring up and down ladders to study frescoes in dimly lit cathedrals must have caused them some amusement. Cassatt coped with whatever loneliness she might have experienced by the rigorous regimen she imposed upon herself. She also found time to travel to Spain, visiting Madrid and Seville. While in Seville she completed a canvas entitled *Pendant le Carnaval*, which was accepted by the Salon of 1872. *Pendant le Carnaval* (Philadelphia Museum of Art) was one of several paintings with Spanish motifs which she produced in the early 1870's, reflecting an interest in such masters as Velasquez, Goya and Murillo as well as such contemporary figures as Manet, whose « Spanish » canvases she had probably seen during her early years in Paris.

Torero and Young Girl (see p. 10) was accepted by the Salon of 1873, an event which must have reassured her that the initial success she had enjoyed with *The Mandolin Player* and *Pendant le Carnaval* was no happy accident. Before returning to Paris to pursue her career in earnest she visited Belgium and the Netherlands to study paintings by Rubens and Hals. One of her studies from this period, a copy of Hals's *Meeting of the Officers of Cluveniers-Doelen* (see p. 9), was a particular favorite of hers. Years later she often was to show this copy to aspiring young artists who would visit her, encouraging them to learn, as she did, from the old masters.

The Paris that greeted Mary Cassatt in 1873 was still reverberating from the shock waves caused by the affair of the « Salon des refusés » a decade earlier. Manet had become, albeit reluctantly, the most controversial and abused artist of the day, the leading exponent of a style of painting which was labeled « ugly and repulsive » by a hostile press and public. Though few realized it at the time, the stranglehold that the Salon had so long held on art was slowly but inexorably being loosened by a handful of artists who were willing to defy convention in the cause of artistic freedom.

One of the more significant manifestations of this new spirit was the opening, in April, 1874, of an exhibition by a group of artists who labeled themselves « The Anonymous Cooperative Society of Artists, Sculptors, Engravers, etc., Endowed with Variable Capital and Personnel, » more familiarly known to us by a pejorative label which eventually stuck: « Impressionists. » The exhibit, which was hung by Renoir in the studio of the photographer Nadar, featured 165 works by 30 artists, including Degas, Monet, Pissarro and Boudin.

Ironically, Manet, who played such an important role in opening the door to modern painting, shied away from joining his more adventuresome contemporaries. « Manet seems determined to remain aloof, » Degas scornfully wrote to a fellow artist whom he sought to recruit for the « Exposition des indépendants. » « I definitely think that he is more vain than intelligent, » he added. *

---

* Degas, E., *Letters*, N° 12, 1874.

Copy after Frans Hals, c. 1873.   Oil on canvas, 18¼" × 28½" (46.3 × 72.3 cm)
Collection: Mrs. Percy C. Madeira Jr., Berwyn, Pennsylvania

10

A Musical Party
1874
Oil on canvas
38″ × 26″
(96.4 × 66 cm)
Museum of the
Petit-Palais, Paris
▷

◁
Torero and
Young Girl, 1873
Oil on canvas
39⅝″ × 33½″
(101.2 × 85.1 cm)
Sterling and
Francine Clark
Art Institute
Williamstown
Massachusetts

11

POPPIES IN A FIELD, c. 1874–1880. Oil on wood, 10½″ × 13⅝″ (26.4 × 34.5 cm)
Philadelphia Museum of Art. Bequest of Charlotte Dorrance Wright

The first exhibition of the Impressionists was well attended, but the members of the press and public who crowded into the second-floor studio in the Rue Dannou were either amused or unfailingly hostile, and the venture was by no means a commercial success.

If the Impressionists were generally ignored and seldom patronized at the onset of their careers, one might well wonder how they survived. The image of the starving artist who lives on little but inspiration is truly more romantic fiction than fact. As an artist of independent means, Cassatt was the exception rather than the rule, and even Degas, whose lineage was aristocratic, was all but impoverished by a family debt.

Credit for the initial survival of the Impressionists must go in large part to the dealer Paul Durand-Ruel, who sustained many of them at a time when there were few buyers to be found, and who hosted two group shows and a number of solo exhibits in his Paris gallery.

At one point he was threatened with bankruptcy, and only Cassatt's timely intervention helped save him. She also helped to find him buyers among her countrymen, by referring clients and by encouraging him to sell in the United States.

Durand-Ruel did arrange for the first exhibition of Impressionist art in the United States in 1886, and opened a gallery two years later in New York. Although his faith in the Impressionist was eventually vindicated, his early support was an act of rare courage and insight. It is characteristic of the milieu in which Cassatt found herself that she and Degas should become acquainted with each other through their art long before they were to actually meet in person. «How well I remember... seeing for the first time Degas' pastels in the window of a picture dealer on the Boulevard Haussmann,» she recalled years later. «I used to go and flatten my nose against that window and absorb all I could of his art. It changed my life.»

Given her intense interest in contemporary art, Cassatt was probably among the crowds who attended the first Impressionist exhibition. Unlike the majority of the people in attendance, she did not go to scoff. She went to learn.

Though he no longer submitted work to the Salon, Degas was interested enough in the 1874 exhibition to stroll through the Salon's galleries one day in the company of his friend Joseph Tourny. Tourny had met Cassatt when both were studying Hals's work in Haarlem, and may have first called Degas' attention to a lively and engaging canvas by Cassatt entitled *Portrait of Madame Cortier* (1874, Maxwell Galleries, San Francisco). Degas was impressed. «C'est vrai,» he remarked to Tourny, «Voilà quelqu'un qui sent comme moi.»*

Three years would pass before Degas, again in the company of Tourny, would call upon Cassatt at her studio. Whether by design or by accident, his timing proved to be perfect.

Cassatt made another important and lasting acquaintance during this period, when she was introduced to Louisine Waldron Elder, a young American who was attending a fashionable Parisian finishing school. Later, as Mrs. Henry O. Havemeyer, the wife of a prominent American industrialist and art collector, she recalled that first meeting:

> «I remember that when I was a young girl... a lady came
> to visit Madame del Satre, where I was a pensionnaire, and I heard
> her say that she could not remain to tea because she was going
> to Courbet's studio to see a picture he had just completed and then
> she spoke of him as a painter of such great ability that I at once
> conceived a curiosity to see some of his pictures.»

------

* «It's true. There is someone who feels as I do.»

Though there was an age difference of more than ten years between them, the two became fast friends, and Louisine Elder quickly came to share her fellow American's enthusiasm for French art:

> « I was about sixteen years old when I first heard of Degas, of course through Miss Cassatt. She took me to see one of his pastels* and advised me to buy it... it was so new and strange to me! I scarcely knew how to appreciate it, or whether I liked it or not, for I believe it takes special brain cells to understand Degas. There was nothing the matter with Miss Cassatt's brain cells, however, and she left me in no doubt as to the desirability of the purchase and I bought it on her advice.»

As Cassatt's appreciation for the new art grew and began to manifest itself in her work, it was almost inevitable that she should eventually run afoul of the Salon's conventions. In 1875 she submitted two canvases, one of which was evidently rejected because it was too bright. She carefully toned down the background, submitted it the following year, and saw her suspicions confirmed when the painting was accepted by the Salon of 1876.

This incident must have convinced her that she could no longer avoid the choice between her principles and the dictates of the Salon. From our present perspective such a decision would not appear terribly difficult, but it must be remembered that Cassatt was preparing to break from the one institution which imparted legitimacy to an artist's work. Without its support she had no reason to expect that she could successfully continue her professional career.

In 1876 and 1877 the Impressionists continued to exhibit their work, courageous acts in light of the lack of popular and financial support with which they had to contend. We may be almost certain that Cassatt attended these showings and that they probably inspired her to try her hand at *plein air* painting. One small oil from this period, *Poppies in a Field* (see p. 12), is highly reminiscent of similar works by Monet and Renoir, suggesting that she had reached the final phase of her transition from academic painting to a style which was frankly imitative of Impressionism. Such a transition is especially notable when one compares *Poppies in a Field* with *A Musical Party* (see p. 11), which was executed approximately one year earlier.

It should be pointed out that artists did not necessarily place as great a degree of emphasis on originality in Cassatt's day as they do at present, and it was perfectly acceptable to work under the influence of a *maître* as long as one did him justice. Her borrowing of stylistic elements was not merely slavish imitation; in each case — and there were many — she carefully analyzed the work of artists whom she admired, and subsequently employed those elements compatible with her own style, thereby producing a distinctive body of work while synthesizing influences from a number of different sources.

Her union with the Impressionist cause was made official by Degas' imprimatur. He visited her studio one afternoon in 1877 and invited her to join the Independents.** Cassatt herself described that fateful meeting to Segard:

---

* The pastel was a *Répétition de Ballet*, and is believed to be the first example of Impressionist art to enter the United States.
** Degas thoroughly detested the term « Impressionist » and never applied it to himself.

In the Omnibus, c. 1891
Preliminary drawing for the print, crayon and pencil on paper, 14³/₈" × 10⁵/₈" (36.5 × 27 cm)
National Gallery of Art, Washington, D.C. The Rosenwald Collection

«I accepted with joy. Finally I would be able to work with absolute independence and without concern for the eventual judgment of a jury! I already knew who my masters were. I admired Manet, Courbet and Degas. I rejected conventional art. I began to live...»*

This meeting began a long and close association between Degas and Cassatt, one based on mutual respect and a shared affinity for beauty and culture. While other artists withered at Degas' waspish epigrams, the spirit, intelligence and talent of the American *mademoiselle* earned his unfailing admiration. In her memoirs, Louisine Havemeyer recalled a conversation in which she pressed her friend for details of Degas' personality:

«Tell me more about him.»

«Oh my dear, he is dreadful! He dissolves your will power,» she said. «Even the painter Moreau said to Degas after years of friendship, that he could no longer stand his attacks: "Voyons, Degas, il faut que je mène ma vie! que nous ne nous voyons plus!"»**

«I led her on to tell me more by asking, "How could you get on with him?"»

«Oh,» she answered, «I am independent! I can live alone and I love to work. Sometimes it made him furious that he could not find a chink in my armor, and there would be months when we just could not see each other, and then something I painted would bring us together again and he would go to Durand-Ruel's and say something nice about me, or come to see me himself. When he saw my *Boy before the Mirror* (see p. 83), he said to Durand-Ruel: "Where is she? I must see her at once. It is the greatest picture of the century." When I saw him he went over all of the details of the picture with me and expressed great admiration for it, and then, as if regretting what he had said, he relentlessly added: "It has all of your qualities and all of your faults — c'est l'Enfant Jésus et sa bonne anglaise."»***

Cassatt was perceptive enough to see beneath Degas' cynical and assured manner a sensitive human being whose uncompromising standards would not allow him to be less than totally honest, however great the cost. Both had devoted their lives to art and each recognized in the other the implicit rewards and sacrifices of such devotion.

One of Degas' more prosaic and revealing letters concerns an errand he undertook on behalf of his American protégée. It is addressed to «M. Le Compte Lepic, supplier of good dogs,» and asks him to find «this distinguished person, whose friendship I honor,» a Belgium griffon from his kennel. «It is a young dog that she needs,» added Degas, «so that he may love her.»****

---

* Segard, A., *op cit.*, p. 8.
** «See here, Degas, I must lead my life! Let us no longer meet!»
*** «...it is the Infant Jesus and His English Nurse.»
**** Degas, E., *op. cit.*, N° 131, undated.

WOMAN AND CHILD DRIVING, 1879. Oil on canvas, 35¼″ × 51½″ (89.3 × 130.8 cm)
Philadelphia Museum of Art. Purchased: The W. P. Wilstach Collection

Woman Reading (Lydia Cassatt), 1878. Oil on canvas, 32″ × 25½″ (81.3 × 64.7 cm)
Norton Simon Foundation, Los Angeles

READING «LE FIGARO», 1883. Oil on canvas, 41″ × 33″ (104 × 83.7 cm)
Private Collection

MOTHER ABOUT TO WASH HER SLEEPY CHILD, 1880.
Oil on canvas, 39½″ × 25¾″ (100 × 65.5 cm)
Los Angeles County Museum of Art. Bequest of Mrs. Fred Hathaway Bixby

Nursing, c. 1891. Drypoint, 9¼" × 6¹⁵/₁₆" (23.5 × 17.6 cm)
The Metropolitan Museum of Art, New York
Bequest of Mrs. H.O. Havemeyer. The H.O. Havemeyer Collection

Like many committed bachelors, Degas could be plainly stuffy about women at times, and it took Cassatt to put him in his place. One anecdote she shared with Segard reveals how deftly she countered one of his maddeningly condescending gestures, not with tears or arguments, but with action. As they were looking at a painting by a mutual friend one day, she remarked that it had no style. Degas began to laugh and shrugged his shoulders as if to say, « Just look at these women who presume to pass an opinion on art! Do they really imagine they know what "style" is? »

The gesture stung, and prompted Cassatt to devise a plan which would teach her mentor not to underestimate the opposite sex. « She found a very ugly model, » relates Segard, « a sort of vulgar looking servant. She had her pose in a shift next to her dressing table, in the act of a woman preparing to retire... the expression is stupid... »

When Degas saw the resultant painting, *Girl Arranging her Hair* (see p. 48), he quickly forgot his misgivings about women: « What drawing! What style! » * he wrote to Cassatt without irony, and promptly acquired it for himself. It remained with him until his death.

Several years later, while admiring a series of color prints Cassatt had executed for her first solo show, Degas again allowed his prejudice to manifest itself, but in this instance at his own expense: « I am not willing to admit that a woman can draw that well, » he remarked to a friend.

The year 1877 proved to be significant for Cassatt in more ways than she might have anticipated. While members of her family had been to Paris to visit her, it is unlikely that she had planned to have them on hand permanently. Nonetheless, Robert Simpson Cassatt, Mrs. Cassatt and Mary's older sister, Lydia, left Philadelphia for Paris, where Mr. Cassatt had decided to retire. Though she was a dutiful daughter and sister and loved her family deeply, Cassatt may have felt a twinge of resentment at the additional burden their care thus imposed upon her. For the next eighteen years she would be forced to cope with the responsibilities of running a household and advancing her career.

The correspondence that passed back and forth between Cassatt's parents and her brothers, who had remained in the United States, speak of her career and the attendant recognition she received in proud, if somewhat bemused tones, as if they still had trouble taking her career seriously. She also kept encouraging her brothers to invest in art, but aside from a few purchases by Alexander, her efforts were to little avail. In plain fact the Cassatts did not know quite what to make of Mary. She remained largely a curiosity to her family, a much-beloved but slightly eccentric spinster who was driven by some force which they could not understand.

In the late 1870's Cassatt began to produce a body of work which clearly demonstrated the extent of her break from the academic traditions of the Salon and her grasp of the lessons she had been learning from Degas and others. Two paintings dated 1878, *Woman Reading (Lydia Cassatt)* (see p. 18) and *Little Girl in a Blue Armchair* (see p. 5) set the stage for what would become increasingly familiar themes: young women or children in relaxed and quiet poses. In the case of Lydia, the brushwork and color are still in the Impressionist mode, though the strong diagonal line of the sitter's body gives us a hint of Cassatt's subsequent passion for structure in her compositions.

---

* Segard, A., *op. cit.*, pp. 184–185.

Drawing for «Portrait of an Old Woman Kritting», c. 1881.
Pencil on paper, 11½" × 8¾" (29.2 × 22.2 cm)
The Metropolitan Museum of Art, New York. Gift of Mrs. Joseph du Vivier

Little Girl in a Blue Armchair is especially noteworthy as it is (to our knowledge) the only work by Cassatt upon which Degas himself worked. In a letter to the dealer Ambroise Vollard, she described the painting and commented on Degas' contribution:

« It was the portrait of a child of a friend of Mr. Degas. I had done the child in the armchair and he found it good and advised me on the background and he even worked on it. I sent it to the American section of the big exposition (1878) and they refused it. As Mr. Degas had found it to be good, I was furious, all the more so since he had worked on it. At that time this appeared new and the jury consisted of three people of which one was a pharmacist! » *

Perhaps the most striking thing about this painting is its use of negative space: the irregularly shaped gray peninsula which thrusts its way through the blue armchairs in the foreground. While the brushwork, particularly in the pattern of the upholstery, is handled loosely, one would have to stretch the definition of the term « Impressionist » to label it as such. Both her study of the old masters and the influence of Degas, himself a modern disciple of Ingres, would not permit her to totally abandon draftsmanship in favor of sensory impressions.

It is reasonable to assume that Degas influenced Cassatt's choice of media as well as her style of painting, for both artists executed a number of works in pastel. They appreciated the freedom that pastel allowed as well as the richness that could be attained by building up successive layers of color. Ever anxious to extend the limits of his medium, Degas performed a number of experiments with pastel, such as moistening it with steam or with turpentine to achieve an impasto-like effect. He and Cassatt both began to apply fixative to their work at various stages of development in order to keep the layers of color purer and more intense. This technique, notes Breeskin, also helped to make their pastels « more durable than those of less knowledgeable artists for whom the medium is likely to be fragile and chalky. » **

If we wish to find a suitable example of Degas' influence on Cassatt at the onset of their relationship, we need look no further than her pastel (c. 1879) entitled *Lydia Leaning on her Arms, Seated in a Loge* (see p. 37). *Lydia* was one of a series of drawings and paintings she executed of women at the theater, and employs a number of devices which become increasingly familiar in her later work: the strong diagonal line of the sitter's body, the use of a mirror to show the figure from two angles simultaneously, and the interplay between the curves of the chair and the curving lines of the body. It is the vibrant color and lively yet controlled use of pastel, however, which most clearly reveals Cassatt's debt to her mentor.

A comparison of *Lydia* with *At the Opera* (see p. 35), painted a year later, reminds us of Cassatt's remark to Segard concerning her masters. She had not entirely given up Manet's influence in favor of Degas. Unlike the Impressionists both Cassatt and Degas used black in their palettes, and her bold use of black in the form of the woman (and the sketchy treatment of the background figures) can be traced to similar works by Manet. Cassatt's conscious use of *repoussoir* is clearly revealed in the preliminary drawing (see p. 36) for this work.

---

* Vollard, A., *Recollections of a Picture Dealer*, p. 180.
** *Mary Cassatt, Pastels and Color Prints*, Exhibition catalogue, p. 17.

A Cup of Tea, 1880. Oil on canvas, 25½″ × 36½″ (64.7 × 92.7 cm)
Museum of Fine Arts, Boston. The Mary Hopkins Fund

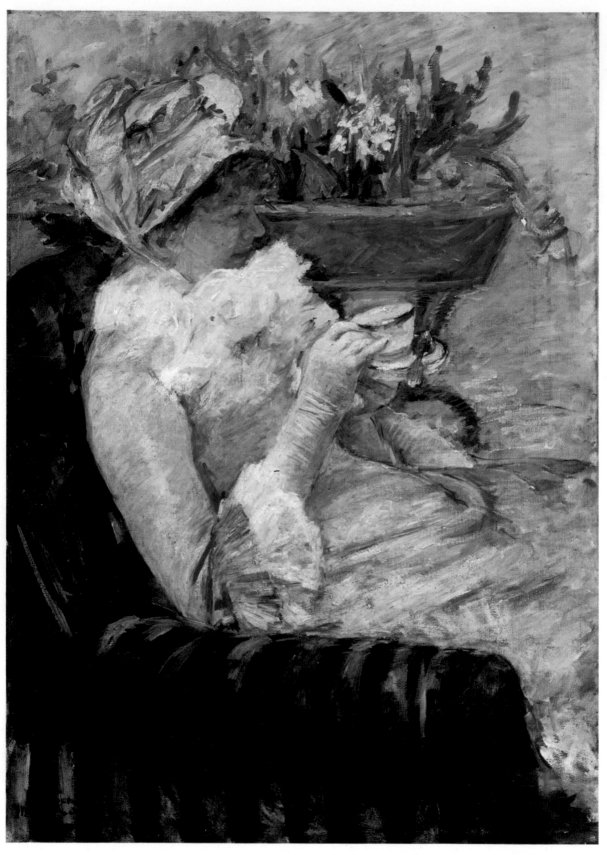

THE CUP OF TEA, 1879. Oil on canvas, 36⅜″ × 25¾″ (92.3 × 65.5 cm)
The Metropolitan Museum of Art, New York. Anonymous Gift

PROFILE PORTRAIT OF LYDIA CASSATT, 1880. Oil on canvas, 38″ × 26″ (93 × 66 cm)
Museum of the Petit-Palais, Paris

WOMAN WITH A DOG
1883
Oil on canvas
39⁷/₁₆″ × 26⁵/₈″
(100.3 × 67.7 cm)
Corcoran Gallery of Art
Washington, D.C.
▷

◁
LADY AT THE TEA TABLE
1883–1885
Oil on canvas
29″ × 24″
(73.4 × 61 cm)
The Metropolitan
Museum of Art
New York
Gift of the Artist

29

LYDIA CROCHETING IN THE GARDEN AT MARLY, 1880
Oil on canvas, 26″ × 37″ (66 × 94 cm)
The Metropolitan Museum of Art, New York. Gift of Mrs. Gardner Cassatt

LYDIA WORKING AT A TAPESTRY FRAME, c. 1881
Oil on canvas, 25¾" × 36¼" (65.5 × 92 cm)
Flint Museum of Arts, Flint, Michigan. Gift of the Whiting Foundation

YOUNG WOMAN SEWING IN A GARDEN, c. 1886.   Oil on canvas, 36″ × 25½″ (91.5 × 64.7 cm)
Jeu de Paume Museum, Paris

Two other paintings from this period suggest Cassatt's affinity for themes centered around the languid rituals of women. *The Cup of Tea* (see p. 26) is stylistically reminiscent of *Woman Reading*. The soft colors and fluid brushwork show further development of the Impressionist influence. *A Cup of Tea* (see p. 25) is much more tightly modeled and is more representative of what was becoming Cassatt's mature style. The familiar figure of Lydia is once again present, but in this instance is accented by the woman on the right, whose face Cassatt has boldly concealed behind a tea cup. The vertical lines of the wallpaper and the flowered chintz of the sofa add pattern and rhythm, as do the lines of the oddly tilted tea service (still in the possession of the Cassatt family) and the curve of the mantel.

A Cup of Tea was shown in the fifth Impressionist exhibit and was the subject of some favorable attention from critic J. K. Huysmans:*

> «It remains for me now, having arrived at the work of M. Degas which I saved for the end, to speak of the two lady painters of the group, Miss Cassatt and Madame Morizot [sic]. A pupil of Degas, Miss Cassatt is evidently also a pupil of English painters, for her excellent canvas, two women taking tea in an interior, reminds me of certain works shown in 1878 in the English section.
>
> «Here it is still the bourgeoisie, but it is no longer like that of M. Caillebotte; it is a world also at ease but more harmonious, more elegant. In spite of her personality, which is still not completely free, Miss Cassatt has nevertheless a curiosity, a special attraction, for a flutter of feminine nerves passes through her painting that is more poised, more peaceful, more capable than that of Mrs. Morizot, a pupil of Manet.»

The period 1879–1880 was a busy one for Cassatt. In addition to her rigorous daily regimen of painting and attending to the needs of her household, she began preparations to join Degas and several of the Impressionists in their plans to publish a journal of original prints, to be called «Le Jour et La Nuit.» With the characteristic enthusiasm and energy with which she undertook all new ventures, she set to work at once. «Mlle Cassatt is trying her hand at engravings,» Degas wrote to Pissarro in 1880, «They are charming.»** Degas himself, however, began to waver. «We must discuss the journal,» he wrote to Felix Bracquemond. «Pissarro and I together made various attempts of which one by Pissarro is a success. At the moment Miss Cassatt is full of it. Impossible for me with my living to earn, to devote myself entirely to it yet.»***

The end result was that «Le Jour et La Nuit» was never published, but the preparations did at least allow Cassatt to reacquaint herself with the techniques of intaglio printmaking, a medium which she had largely ignored since her studies with Carlo Raimondi in Parma nearly ten years before.

With *Woman and Child Driving* (see p. 17) Cassatt began to employ the asymmetry and severe cropping which Degas favored in his compositions. Lydia is depicted driving a carriage, accompanied by a little girl (Odile Fèvre, one of Degas' nieces) and a groom, whom

---

* Huysmans, J. K., *L'art moderne*, p. 112.
** Degas, E., *op. cit.*, No 33, 1880.
*** *ibidem*, No 31, 1879–1880.

PORTRAIT OF A YOUNG WOMAN IN BLACK, 1883. Oil on canvas, 31½″ × 25¼″ (80 × 64 cm)
On permanent loan from the Peabody Institute to the Baltimore Museum of Art

#1 Lydia leaning on her arms , seated in a Loge

*Sa soeur Lydia est representée dans une pose informal , tordé dans une direction pendant qu'elle regarde la scène.

*Les coup de pinceau sont lourds et le contour est bien défini.

*Les couleurs sur les épaule et sur les cheveax sont claires parce-que la lumière est artificelle.

AT THE OPERA, 1880. Oil on canvas, 32″ × 26″ (81.3 × 66 cm)
Museum of Fine Arts, Boston. The Charles Henry Hayden Fund

Study for «At the Opera», 1880. Soft pencil on paper, 4″ × 6″ (10.2 × 15.3 cm)
Museum of Fine Arts, Boston. Gift of Dr. Hans Schaetter

Lydia Leaning on her Arms, Seated in a Loge, c. 1879. Pastel on paper, 21⅝″ × 17¾″ (55 × 45 cm)
Nelson Atkins Museum, Kansas City, Missouri. Anonymous Gift

we see only in profile. Though the subjects are ostensibly in the act of motion, their dour expressions and stiff poses resemble not so much a spontaneous, joyous outing as a carefully composed and self-conscious family photograph.

The theme that is most frequently associated with Cassatt — maternity — is one that first appeared in 1880, and seems to coincide with a lengthy visit from her older brother and his family. While Alexander Cassatt and his wife remained in Paris, their four children spent a good part of the summer with their aunts and grandparents in the country, at Marly-le-Roi. No doubt the older Cassatts were delighted to see their grandchildren, and « Aunt Mary » took advantage of the occasion to execute a number of paintings and drawings of her nieces and nephews as well as a formal portrait of her brother.

From this period comes *Mother about to Wash her Sleepy Child* (see p. 20), generally regarded as Cassatt's first comprehensive treatment of the mother-and-child theme, and a work that beautifully captures the exuberance and freshness of youth. Like Whistler, whom she knew and admired, Cassatt was intrigued by the variations which could be attained within a given value, usually white. *Mother about to Wash her Sleepy Child* is but one of a number of paintings thus analyzed.

The interruptions of her nieces and nephews did not keep Cassatt from taking advantage of the fine summer weather to complete two excellent portraits of her sister, *Lydia Crocheting in the Garden at Marly* (see p. 30) and *Profile Portrait of Lydia* (see p. 27). Degas was evidently pleased by her progress, for that October he wrote a friend, « The Cassatts have come back from Marly. Mlle Cassatt is settling in a ground floor studio which does not seem too healthy to me. What she did in the country looks very well in the studio light. It is much stronger and nobler than what she had last year. »

On April 2, 1881, the sixth group exhibition opened and was again reviewed by Huysmans. Though generally critical of the Impressionists he was unstinting in his praise of Cassatt:

> « I wrote last year that most of Miss Cassatt's canvases recalled the pastels of Degas and one of them derived from modern English masters.
>
> « From these two influences has come an artist who owes nothing any longer to anyone, an artist wholly spontaneous and personal. Her exhibition is composed of children, interiors, gardens, and it is a miracle how in these subjects, so much cherished by the English, Miss Cassatt has known the way to escape from sentimentality on which most of them have foundered, in all their work written or painted.
>
> « Oh! those babies, good heavens, how their portraits can exasperate me! Such a crew of English and French daubers have painted them in such stupid and pretentious poses!
>
> « For the first time, thanks to Miss Cassatt, I have seen effigies of ravishing youngsters, quiet bourgeois scenes painted with a delicate and charming tenderness...
>
> « Two other pictures, one called *The Garden** where in the foreground a woman reads while on a diagonal behind her there

---

* *Lydia Crocheting in the Garden at Marly.*

38

are masses of green dotted with red geraniums with a border of dark Chinese nettles extending as far as the house. The other, called *Tea*, in which a woman dressed in pink, smiling, seated in an armchair, holds a teacup in her gloved hands, adding to this tender, contemplative note the fine sense of Parisian elegance. And it is a special indication of her talent that Miss Cassatt, who, I believe, is an American, paints French women for us. But in houses so Parisian she puts the friendly smile of an "at home." She achieves in Paris something that none of our painters could express, the happy contentment, the quiet friendliness of an interior.» *

It was typical of Cassatt not to allow such praise to turn her head. Ambroise Vollard made a special point of noting her aversion to «pushing» her work in public. «One day at an exhibition,» he wrote, «they were fighting for and against the Impressionists.

«"But," said someone, speaking to Mary Cassatt without knowing who she was, "you are forgetting a foreign painter that Degas ranks very high."

«"Who is that?" she asked in astonishment.

«"Mary Cassatt."

«Without false modesty, quite naturally, she exclaimed, "Oh, nonsense!"

«"She is jealous," murmured the other, turning away.» **

The exhibition of 1881, while encouraging from Cassatt's point of view, was marred by increasing acrimony among the participants, many of whom took umbrage at Degas' high-handed manner. «This man (Degas) has gone sour,» complained Caillebotte in a letter to Pissarro. «He doesn't hold the big place he ought according to his talent and, although he will never admit it, he bears the whole world a grudge.» ***

As a result of the dispute — most of it centered around the question of membership in the seventh exhibition — several artists refused to participate, choosing instead to return to the Salon. Pissarro tried in vain to keep peace among the warring factions, but the arguments rose to such a pitch that Degas finally announced he would not participate, and Cassatt loyally joined him.

On November 7, 1882, her beloved sister Lydia died from Bright's disease, a kidney infection which had plagued her for years. It is fitting that Cassatt's last painting of her sister, *Lydia Working at a Tapestry Frame* (see p. 31), is also her finest, a masterpiece of color and composition. It is a work of subtle contrasts, the tightly modeled upper half of the canvas set off by the loose and sketchy quality of the lower, the light from the window on the left balanced by the dark form of the dresser on the right.

In the final analysis *Lydia Working at a Tapestry Frame* captivates us not by subtleties of composition, however, but for the same reason that we are captivated by Vermeer's ability to capture a luminous moment in time. It is an outstanding tribute to the patient and gentle nature of Lydia Cassatt, who so frequently served as a model for her sister.

Lydia's death brought Alexander Cassatt and his family back to France once again, a visit that on this occasion was clouded by grief. Cassatt coped with her sorrow in the only way she knew, through her work.

---

* Huysmans, J. K., *op. cit.*, pp. 231–234.
** Vollard, A., *op. cit.*, p. 181.
*** Rewald, J., *History of Impressionism*, p. 348.

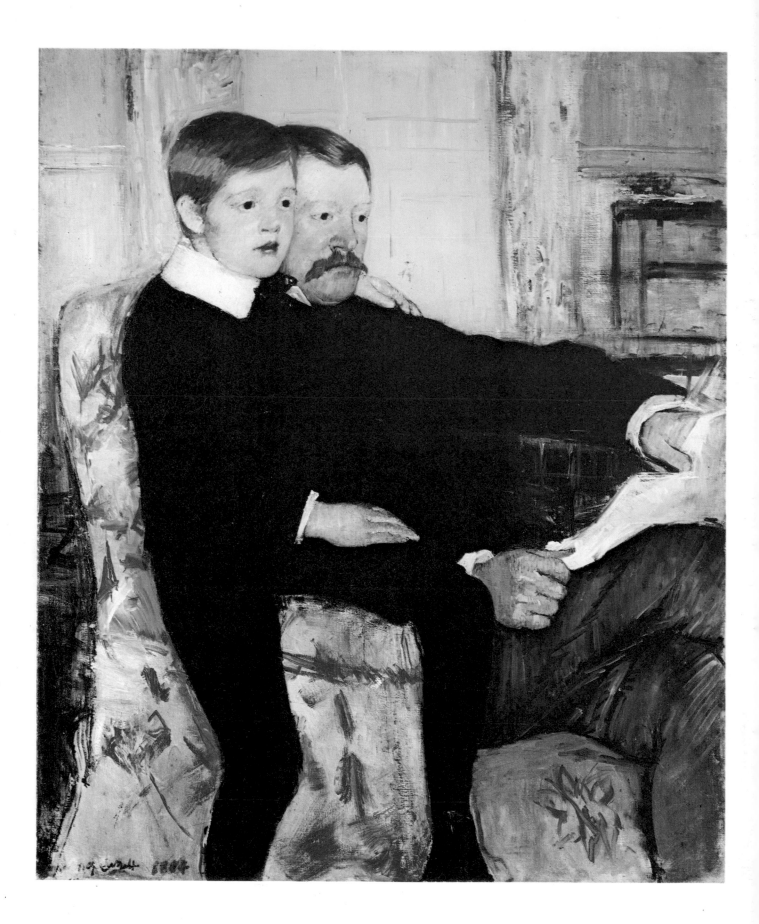

◁

Céleste Seated on a Park Bench, c. 1899. Drypoint, II final state, 11″ × 7″ (28 × 17.7 cm)
Philadelphia Museum of Art
Gift of R. Sturgis, Frederic Ballard, Alexander Cassatt, Staunton B. Peck, and Mrs. William Potter Wear

Reflection, c. 1890. Drypoint, V state, 10¼" × 6¹⁵/₁₆" (26 × 17.6 cm)
The Metropolitan Museum of Art, New York
Bequest of Mrs. H.O. Havemeyer. The H.O. Havemeyer Collection

Mary Cassatt

THE SISTERS, c. 1885. Oil on canvas, 18¼″ × 21⅞″ (46.2 × 56 cm)
Glasgow Art Gallery

◁
Jeannette in a Floppy Hat Leaning against a Chair, c. 1904
Drypoint, 8½″ × 5⅞″ (21.5 × 15 cm)
Philadelphia Museum of Art
Gift of Mrs. Charles P. Davis and Gardner Cassatt in memory of Mary Cassatt

46

THE FAMILY
1887
Oil on canvas
32″ × 26″
(81.2 × 66 cm)
Chrysler Museum
at Norfolk
Virginia

MOTHER AND
CHILD, c. 1890
Oil on canvas
35⅜″ × 25⅜″
(90 × 64.4 cm)
Wichita Art
Museum, Kansas
The Roland
P. Murdock
Collection

#2. Girl arranging her hair

*La peinture s'appelle Girl arranging her hair.

* Elle a peint Girl arranging her hair en 1886.

* C'est une portrait d'une femme domestique.

* La lumière est vèrtiable.

* Il y a des contours sur la peinture.

*Les coup de pinceau sont lourds et les couleurs sont claires.

48

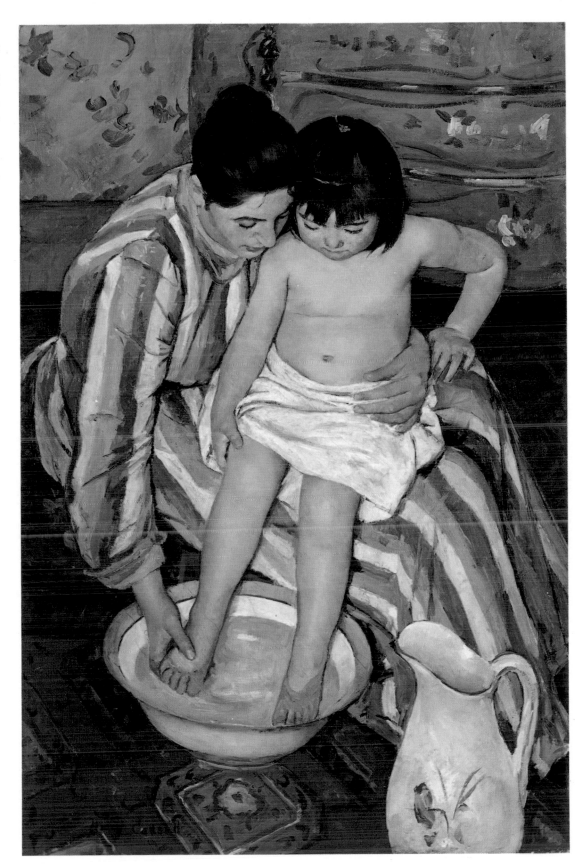

THE BATH
c. 1891
Oil on canvas
39½″ × 26″
(100.3 × 66 cm)
Art Institute
of Chicago
The Robert
A. Waller Fund
▷

◁
GIRL ARRANGING
HER HAIR
1886
Oil on canvas
29½″ × 24½″
(75 × 62.2 cm)
National Gallery
of Art
Washington, D.C.
Chester Dale
Collection

WOMAN WITH A RED ZINNIA, 1891. Oil on canvas, 29″ × 23¾″ (73 × 60.5 cm)
National Gallery of Art, Washington, D.C. Chester Dale Collection

YOUNG WOMEN PICKING FRUIT, 1891. Oil on canvas, 52″ × 36″ (132 × 91.5 cm)
Museum of Art, Carnegie Institute, Pittsburgh, Pennsylvania

LILACS IN A WINDOW, c. 1889. Oil on canvas, 24¼″ × 20″ (61.6 × 51 cm). Private Collection

«How we try for happiness, poor things,» she wrote to Louisine Havemeyer years later, «and how we don't find it; the best cure is hard work — if only one has the health for it you do that.» From her brother's visit came several drawings and prints of her nephews and nieces, particularly nine-year-old Robbie, and yet another portrait of Alexander Cassatt.

Cassatt was soon left in search of other models, and she therefore turned to the household staff for help. *Susan Seated Outdoors* (see front cover) and *Woman with a Dog* (see p. 29) are two fine paintings of a young woman believed to be the cousin of Mathilde Vallet, Cassatt's faithful housekeeper.

Cassatt's mother is the subject of one of her finest portraits, entitled *Reading Le Figaro* (see p. 19), completed in 1883. It is particularly daring in the severely limited palette which she employed, and suggests that Whistler's experiments in a similar vein (his famous *Portrait of the Artist's Mother* was displayed at the Paris Salon in 1883) may have inspired this dramatic departure from her usual tonality.

Another stylish oil from this period is *Portrait of a Young Woman in Black* (see p. 34).

One portrait that Cassatt began late in 1883 was not completed until two years later, and was not well received by the sitter's family. *Lady at the Tea Table* (see p. 28), a portrait of Mrs. Robert Moore Riddle (a first cousin of Mrs. Robert Simpson Cassatt), was originally painted to acknowledge a gift of Canton blue china that the Cassatts had received from Mrs. Riddle's daughter. It is a masterfully executed and insightful study, but the family, whom Mrs. Cassatt described as «not very artistic,» took an instant dislike to the portrait, maintaining that the nose was out of proportion.

Though modest enough by nature, Cassatt did not take kindly to criticism from amateurs. She hid the canvas away in a closet where it remained until it was subsequently discovered by Mrs. Havemeyer. She recognized its quality and insisted that it be exhibited, predicting (correctly) that it would receive the praise it deserved.

This incident may have helped to reinforce Cassatt's aversion to commissioned works. Years later she did relent and painted several commissioned portraits in pastel, but she preferred to use members of her family or anonymous peasant women and their children as models.

Thanks to some success in the sales of her paintings and financial support from her brother Alexander, Cassatt could afford time away from her work, a situation which became increasingly common as her mother's health deteriorated. Mrs. Cassatt suffered greatly from a weak heart and rheumatism, and in the hopes of improving her condition she and her daughter escaped from the winter cold of Paris in 1883. They headed for the southern coast of Spain and remained there until the following spring.

Further interruptions resulted from the need to find suitable quarters in Paris, so that 1884 proved to be a most unproductive year. Cassatt did find time to sit for a portrait by Degas (coll. André Meyer, New York), but she was disappointed in the result and secretly sought to dispose of it. Unlike Mrs. Riddle's daughter she was not about to share her disappointment with the artist.

Toward the end of 1884 her brother Alexander and nephew Robert made another of their frequent visits, and Cassatt took advantage of their presence to execute a rare double portrait of father and son (see p. 40).

In *Lydia Working at a Tapestry Frame*, Cassatt had literally split the canvas in half, symbolizing the choice that confronted her at the time between Impressionism on the one

BABY ON HIS MOTHER'S ARM, SUCKING HIS FINGER, 1889. Pastel on paper, 25″ × 19″ (63.5 × 48.2 cm)
Louvre Museum, Paris

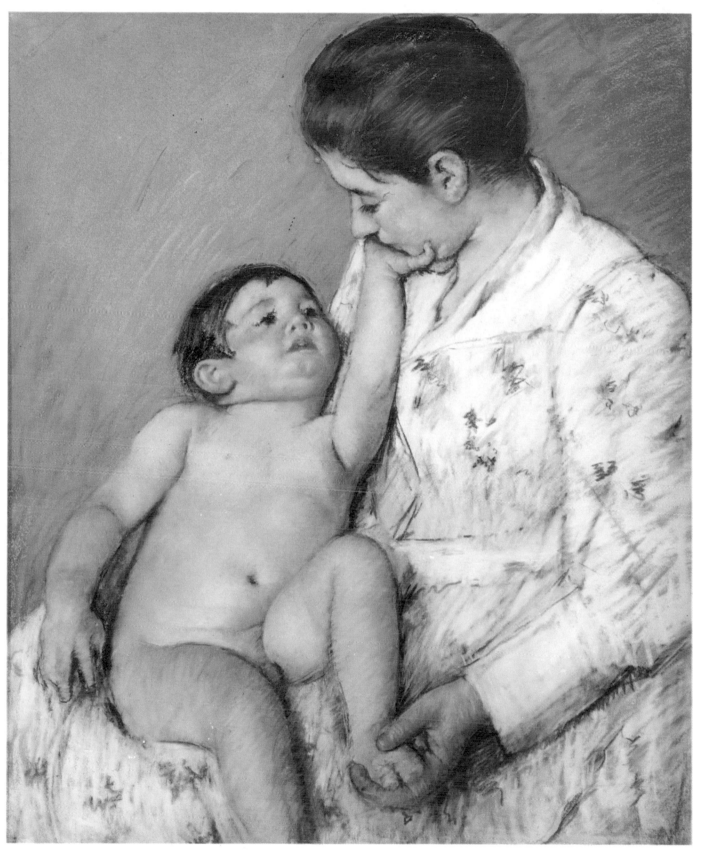

BABY'S FIRST CARESS, 1891. Pastel on paper, 30″ × 24″ (76.2 × 61 cm)
New Britain Museum of American Art, Connecticut. Harriett Russell Stanley Fund

hand and «classicism» on the other. By 1886, when she painted *Young Woman Sewing in the Garden* (see p. 32), *The Family* (see p. 46) and *Girl Arranging her Hair*, she had evidently opted in favor of a «classical» emphasis on form. The firmer modeling of her figures may reveal her interest in the works of Holbein, whom she had come to admire. Certainly her study of the baby in *The Family* suggests all the precision and economy of a Holbein drawing, and the underlying structure in *Girl Arranging her Hair* is plainly visible. Cassatt did retain some elements of Impressionism in her brushwork, but usually employed such brushwork as a foil to the figures which dominated her compositions.

While Durand-Ruel was busy arranging for his major Impressionist exhibit at the American Art Association in New York — the first such exhibit in the United States — Cassatt and her colleagues were feverishly making preparations for the eighth (and last) group show, which opened on May 15, 1886, at a rented studio on the Boulevard des Italiens. Despite the customary bickering among the participants Degas was persuaded to contribute several works, including two pastels in which Cassatt served as the model. The sensation of the exhibit, however, was Seurat's *A Sunday Afternoon on the Island of the Grande Jatte*, which, together with other Pointillist canvases by Signac and Pissarro, brought a predictable wave of public outrage and/or amusement.

Durand-Ruel returned to Paris in late June with the encouraging news that his exhibit had aroused friendly interest among the Americans. Though sales had not been great he agreed with Cassatt that there was an untapped and potentially great market for his artists' work in the United States.

In 1887 Cassatt and her parents moved once again, this time to an apartment at 10, rue de Marignan which featured the amenities of an elevator (considered essential in light of Mrs. Cassatt's bad heart) and central heating. Cassatt kept this apartment as her Paris residence for the rest of her life.

In 1888 her work was interrupted by a riding accident in which she sustained a broken leg and a dislocated shoulder. No doubt the accident was doubly galling: she was an avid horsewoman and was told that further riding was out of the question, and her injuries must have made work of any sort extremely tiresome and painful.

Her output during the period 1887–1890 was relatively small, though she was able to complete several outstanding variations on the mother-and-child theme, among them *Baby on his Mother's Arm* (see p. 54) and *Mother and Child* (see p. 47), as well as a rare still life, *Lilacs in a Window* (see p. 52).

One of the most pronounced influences on late 19th century French art came not out of the mainstream of European civilization but from the island Empire of Japan, which had only recently (since 1853, with the arrival of Commodore Perry's Pacific Squadron in Yedo Harbor) opened its doors to the West. As early as 1862 a shop in the Rue de Rivoli called «La Jonque Chinoise,» run by a Madame De Soye, began to sell examples of oriental art to a growing number of Parisian connoisseurs and collectors — among them Degas — and by 1878 a Japanese pavilion at the Paris World's Fair was attracting huge crowds.

Japanese art proved to be an endless source of fascination and inspiration for the Impressionists. Its refined line and unique concept of space especially appealed to Degas and Cassatt, who began to employ many of its conventions in their work.

In April, 1890, a major exhibition of Japanese prints was held at the Ecole des Beaux-Arts. As might be expected, it had a profound effect on Cassatt. She had been polishing her printmaking skills on and off for over a decade, ever since she had begun to

THE LAMP, 1891
Color print with drypoint, softground and aquatint, 13⅝" × 8¹⁵⁄₁₆" (34.5 × 22.7 cm)
Worcester Art Museum, Massachusetts. Bequest of Mrs. Kingsmill Marrs

The Sick Child, 1889. Drypoint, 5⅝" × 4¾" (14.3 × 12 cm)
Philadelphia Museum of Art

Mother Berthe Holding her Child, 1889. Drypoint, 9³⁄₈″ × 6¹⁄₄″ (24.8 × 16 cm)
Philadelphia Museum of Art

THE LETTER, 1891. Color print with drypoint and aquatint, 13⅝″ × 8¹⁵⁄₁₆″ (34.5 × 22.7 cm)
Bibliothèque Nationale, Paris

The Letter, 1891. Drypoint, I state, 13⁹/₁₆″ × 8¹⁵/₁₆″ (31.4 × 22.8 cm)
The Metropolitan Museum of Art, New York. Gift of Arthur Sachs

THE FITTING, 1891. Color print with drypoint and aquatint, 14¾″ × 10⅛″ (37.5 × 25.7 cm)
Bibliothèque Nationale, Paris

WOMAN BATHING, 1891. Color print with drypoint and aquatint, 14⁵/₁₆″ × 10⁹/₁₀″ (38 × 26.8 cm)
Bibliothèque Nationale, Paris

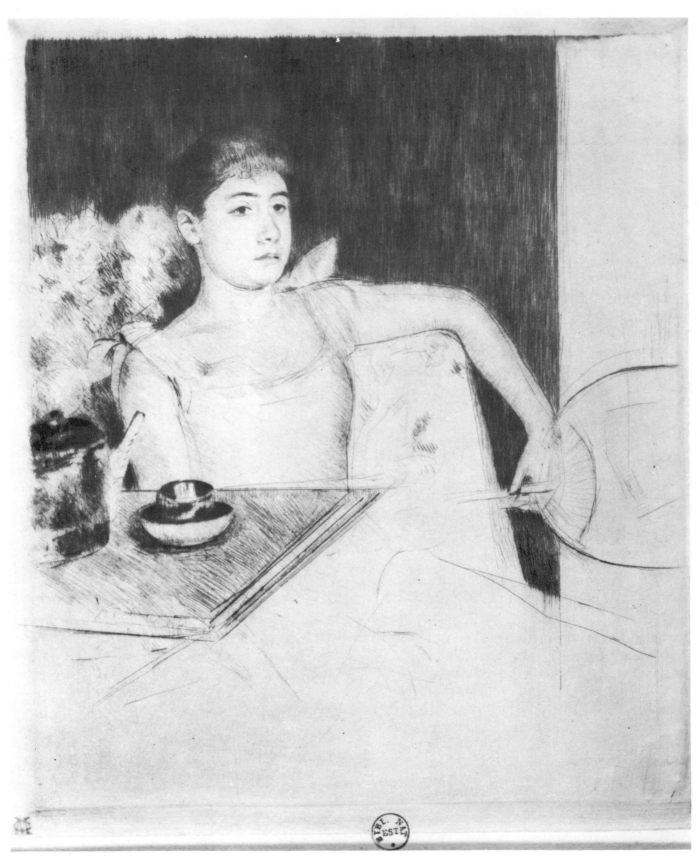

The Tea, 1890. Drypoint, V state, 7¹/₁₆″ × 6⅛″ (18 × 15.5 cm)
Bibliothèque Nationale, Paris

AFTERNOON TEA PARTY, 1891.   Color print with drypoint and aquatint, 13½″ × 18⅛″ (34.4 × 46 cm)
Bibliothèque Nationale, Paris

prepare work for the ill-fated « Le Jour et La Nuit. » The exhibit at the Ecole des Beaux-Arts served to pose an inspirational challenge: could she adapt the sinuous floating line and delicate color of Japanese woodcuts to intaglio?

That summer she rented a studio, engaged a printer named Le Roy to assist her, and set to work. The graphic techniques that she chose to use all come under the general heading of intaglio (Italian: « to cut »), which is probably the most tedious and exacting of the various methods available to produce prints. A smooth metal plate, traditionally copper, is incised either by hand or with the help of acid. Ink is then rubbed into the incised lines and the surface of the plate is wiped clean. When the metal is covered with a slightly damp piece of paper and run through an etching press, the pressure of the rollers in the press squeezes the ink out of the plate and onto the damp paper.

In drypoint, the lines are scratched directly into the plate with a sharp tool. Since the tool acts rather like a plow, it raises a low metal furrow, or « burr, » on either side of the drypoint line. The burr traps some of the ink that is rubbed across the plate and gives drypoint engravings a characteristically soft, almost fuzzy line. (See pp. 72, 77).

In soft-ground etching a preliminary drawing is worked up on a piece of paper and is then placed over a metal plate which has been coated with a soft, acid-resistant substance called a « ground. » When the drawing is traced over with a sharp pencil, ground is pulled off the plate wherever the lines are drawn. The plate is then placed in an acid water bath that literally « eats » away the exposed lines, thus rendering it suitable for printing.

The third intaglio technique which Cassatt used is called aquatint, and is generally used to add tones or textures to a print, rather than lines. In this technique the artist uses an acid-resistant varnish to block out those areas of the metal plate which are not to be etched. He then places the plate, face up, into a box to which a small bellows has been attached. As the bellows is pumped it stirs the air inside the box and fills it with fine grains of rosin which eventually settle and leave a dusty film on the surface of the plate. When the metal is heated, each of the particles of rosin melts and forms a tiny, acid-resistant bead. The printmaker can obtain different tonal values by varying the amount of rosin he uses and by controlling the time that the plate is in the acid bath.

Cassatt described her work in a letter which she wrote to Mr. Samuel Avery of the Metropolitan Museum in 1903:

> «...I have sent with the set of my colored etchings all of the "states" I had. I wish that I could have had more but I had to hurry on and be ready for my printer when I could get him. The printing is a great work; sometimes we worked all day (eight hours) both as hard as we could and we only printed eight or ten proofs in the day. My method is very simple. I drew an outline in drypoint and transferred this to two other plates, making in all three plates, never more, for each proof. Then I put an aquatint wherever the color was to be printed; the color was painted on the plate as it was to appear in the proof...»*

---

* Breeskin notes that the intervening twelve years between the time Cassatt produced her prints and wrote her letter to Avery «...were sufficiently long time to have caused her to forget the important role that soft-ground played in the description of the process.» See exhibition catalogue, *op. cit.*, p. 38.

The result of this considerable labor was a series of ten color prints which formed the centerpiece of the first solo show at Durand-Ruel's in April, 1891. (See pp. 57, 60, 62, 63, 65, 68). This series is justly regarded by Cassatt scholars as an artistic and technical *tour de force*, perhaps her finest single achievement. The challenge of grafting the atmospheric qualities and compositional elements of Japanese graphics onto the world of the European haute bourgeoisie has been achieved with remarkable success, thanks to Cassatt's sensitivity and consummate draftsmanship. It is doubtful whether any other artist of her time would have been capable of such an endeavor.

As if to acknowledge her debt to the art which served as the inspiration for her series of color prints, she added an amusing note by giving several of her models decidedly oriental features, a device which is especially noticeable in *The Letter* (see p. 60).

Cassatt had waited until she was 46 years old before she held her first solo exhibit. She had worked long and hard to prove herself worthy of being considered the equal of her male contemporaries, to demonstrate that gender was for all intents and purposes irrelevant when it came to matters of art. The keen edge of exhilaration and satisfaction that she ought to have felt and so much deserved was dulled, however, by an act of provincialism. A group of artists, many of whom had exhibited with Cassatt in the group shows, formed an organization called the «Société des peintres-graveurs français,» and limited their membership to native Frenchmen. This excluded the American Cassatt as well as Pissarro, who was born in the West Indies. While members of the Société held their group show in the large gallery at Durand-Ruel's, Cassatt and Pissarro simultaneously held individual exhibits of their work in smaller adjacent rooms. The week before their exhibit was to open, Pissarro wrote to his son Lucien:

> «My dear Lucien: It is absolutely necessary, while what I saw yesterday at Miss Cassatt's is still fresh in my mind, to tell you about the colored engravings she is to show at Durand-Ruel's at the same time as I. We open Saturday, the same day as the patriots,* who, between the two of us, are going to be furious when they discover right next to their exhibition a show of rare and exquisite works.»**

Although the four paintings and the series of ten color prints she exhibited received praise from Degas and a few others, sales and critical acclaim were not overwhelming, and a subsequent exhibit in New York proved equally disappointing. Cassatt had had a taste of independence, however, and was now ready to make a name for herself, not as «a pupil of M. Degas,» but as an artist in her own right.

Robert Simpson Cassatt died in December, 1891. Though he was mourned deeply his departure had no practical effect on the Cassatt household, which his daughter had ably managed since her sister and parents had arrived to stay years before.

As was her custom Cassatt found relief from sorrow in her work. Despite the relative success which she enjoyed in France she had sought for years to gain recognition in America

---

* Pissarro used the term sarcastically.
** Pissarro, C., *Letters to his Son Lucien*, ed. John Rewald, p. 158.

GATHERING FRUIT, c. 1893. Color print with drypoint and aquatint, 16¹¹/₁₆″ × 11¹¹/₁₆″ (42.5 × 29.7 cm)
Collection: Mrs. Adelyn D. Breeskin, Washington, D.C.

as well. It is hardly surprising, then, that she accepted a commission to execute a mural for the 1893 Chicago World's Fair when it was offered her. The scale of the mural — which was to be placed on the south tympanum of the Woman's Building — was far larger than any she had hitherto employed, and must have seemed a dramatic departure from the intricate work of the color prints upon which she had spent most of the previous year.

In recognition of their increasingly important role in modern American society, the Woman's Building was to be designed by a woman architect and decorated by woman artists. The subject of Cassatt's assignment was «Modern Woman,» while the tympanum opposite hers, to be painted by Mary Fairchild MacMonnies, was to be labeled «Primitive Woman.»

The idea of climbing up and down scaffolding in order to paint the fifty-foot expanse of canvas designed for the mural struck Cassatt as unnecessary, and she therefore arranged to have a huge trench dug in the floor of her studio. This allowed her to work at ground level and move the canvas up and down as needed. Rather than paint heroic figures in order to fill the allotted space, she designed a rather wide ornamental border and divided the composition into three panels, which she labeled *Young Women Picking the Fruits of Knowledge and Science, Young Girls Pursuing Fame,* and *Music and Dance.*

Whatever hopes and expectations she might have had about her new venture went unrealized. The mural was skied approximately forty feet from ground level so that Cassatt's slightly less than life-sized figures could hardly be appreciated. Even more disturbing to her must have been the news that the murals were either lost or destroyed when the Chicago World's Fair closed. To this day no trace of them has been found.

The Chicago experience was unpleasant enough to keep Cassatt from ever again attempting mural work, though the scale of her paintings did enlarge slightly for a time, most notably in *The Boating Party* (see back cover). One of her best known and most highly regarded canvases, *The Boating Party* was executed while Cassatt and her mother spent the summer of 1894 in the south of France, at Antibes.

Of all her works *The Boating Party* is perhaps the boldest and most imbued with its own *élan vital.* Cassatt has achieved a hitherto unsurpassed degree of success in locking together the large, flat planes of color which distinguish this work. The Van Gogh – like clash of yellow and blue and the severe foreshortening add a jarring note to what is otherwise the model of a family excursion. Although she very likely would have denied it, *The Boating Party* took Cassatt to the farthest limits of her sense of «modernity». The forms have been reduced to their simplest components until it is quite possible to see them as abstractions.

It was Cassatt's practice to seek relief from the city's summer heat by renting a retreat in the country or near the seashore, and a considerable amount of her time each winter and spring was taken up with the business of finding suitable quarters for herself and her family. Accordingly she began to look about for a permanent summer residence, one that would be comfortable and convenient to Paris.

In 1892 she purchased Château Beaufresne, a 17th century manor house in the valley of the Oise, near Beauvais. For the rest of her life she divided most of her time between Château Beaufresne and her apartment on the Rue de Marignan in Paris.

Cassatt's relationship with Degas, meanwhile, had cooled. Even his most loyal friend had come to realize that his caustic remarks could inhibit as well as inspire. The strain was great enough to keep her from seeking his advice while she was working on the murals for the Chicago World's Fair, even though she was sorely tempted to do so. A later incident,

The Stocking, 1890. Drypoint, 10¼" × 7⁵/₁₆" (26 × 18.6 cm)
The Metropolitan Museum of Art, New York
Bequest of Mrs. H.O. Havemeyer. The H.O. Havemeyer Collection

The Bath, 1891. Drypoint, 12⁷/₁₆″ × 9¾″ (31.5 × 24.7 cm)
Philadelphia Museum of Art. Gift of Mrs. Binney Hare

The Parrot, 1891. Drypoint, IV state, 6⅜" × 4¹¹/₁₆" (16.2 × 12 cm)
The Metropolitan Museum of Art, New York. Gift of Arthur Sachs

SLEEPY THOMAS SUCKING HIS THUMB, 1893. Pastel on paper, 21″ × 17½″ (53.3 × 44.5 cm)
Foundation E. G. Bührle, Zurich

in which Degas made a slighting reference to her work through a mutual acquaintance, so hurt her feelings that she stopped seeing him for years thereafter.

The early 1890's saw Cassatt at the height of her creative powers, producing outstanding and original works in rapid succession. *Maternity, With Baby Observing* (coll. Jennipher J. Gregg, Jacksonville, Florida), *Baby's First Caress* (see p. 55), *The Bath* (see p. 49), *In the Garden* (see p. 81), and *Sleepy Thomas, Sucking his Thumb* (see p. 73) all demonstrate that she had not yet exhausted the inherent possibilities of the mother-and-child theme. In *Young Women Picking Fruit* (see p. 51) and *Woman with a Red Zinnia* (see p. 50) Cassatt has depicted women of her generation who, like her, have retained the bloom of healthy vitality.

Her professional career continued to flourish, at least in France. A comprehensive individual show was held at Durand-Ruel's Paris galleries in 1893, and this time consisted of 98 works. The exhibit was successful enough for Cassatt and Durand-Ruel to agree that she was ready for her first solo show in the United States, and two years later her works were hung in Durand-Ruel's newly opened New York gallery. Once again her dream of earning recognition from her countrymen went unrealized; sales were disappointing and attendance was sparse. «I am very much disappointed that my compatriots have so little liking for my work,» she wrote to her friend Mathilda Brownell, expressing a sentiment that for her had become bitterly familiar.

Four days before Christmas, 1895, Mrs. Robert Simpson Cassatt died and was buried beside her husband in a family vault near Château Beaufresne. The heavy mantle of responsibility that Cassatt had so long worn was lifted. She was free at last to do as she pleased. Ironically, the period of her greatest productivity would coincide with the time that she had spent caring for her family. She was fifty-one years old at the time of her mother's death and would live for another thirty years, but after 1895 both her productivity and the quality of her work began to suffer. There were still occasional flashes of the brilliance which she had once demonstrated: *Portrait of a Woman with a Fan* (see p. 78), *Little Anne Sucking her Finger* (see p. 85), and her delightful *Breakfast in Bed* (see p. 84) are examples that unfortunately began to prove the exception rather than the rule.

The void that was left by her mother's death was filled to some extent by the presence of the Havemeyers, who were in Europe in 1895–96, and who no doubt helped to sustain Cassatt in her worst moments. She and Louisine Havemeyer had kept up their friendship over the years since they had first met and were now as close as sisters. The affection that she felt for her own mother is reflected in a tender and engaging pastel portrait of Mrs. Havemeyer and her daughter Electra (coll. Dr. and Mrs. Fletcher McDowell, New York); Cassatt's characteristically detached objectivity is replaced here by a warm and personal statement.

Perhaps the disappointment of her individual show in New York finally convinced her that she would have to make her contribution to the advancement of art in her seemingly indifferent native country by taking a new tack. Rather than seeking success as an artist she would use her taste and influence to help build great public collections of art in the United States. This idea was one that she had espoused before, and one in which she was no doubt encouraged by Louisine Havemeyer.

As if to re-establish old ties with her roots, she suffered the Atlantic crossing in order to visit «home» (which now meant her brothers Alexander and Gardner and their families) in 1898, the first such visit in 28 years. Even then she was not to be spared humiliation at the hands of her countrymen. The «Philadelphia Ledger» greeted her arrival with less than passing interest:

> «Mary Cassatt, sister of Mr. Cassatt, president of the Pennsylvania Railroad, returned from Europe yesterday. She has been studying painting in France and owns the smallest Pekingese [sic] dog in the world.»

Cassatt's reaction to this slight is not recorded, but we may be sure that she had a few choice words to say about the reporter's ignorance of painting and of dogs.

After visiting her family and executing a few commissioned portraits of friends, Cassatt returned to Europe and began making plans to accompany the Havemeyers on a «shopping trip» through Italy and Spain. In 1901 she met them in Genoa and they immediately set off, with Cassatt in the lead. «Miss Cassatt had the "flair" of an old hunter,» wrote Louisine Havemeyer, «and her experience made her as patient as Job and as wise as Solomon in art matters; Mr. Havemeyer had the true energy of a collector while I — well, I had the time of my life.»

Cassatt was prescient enough to realize that Europe was still a bargain hunter's paradise, artistically speaking. If one had the knowledge, money and stamina to ferret out works by masters from various periods, some of whom were not yet in vogue, fantastic bargains could be found. During the ensuing decade she channelled much of the energy that she had devoted to her own work into her role as agent-advisor to the Havemeyers. Upon her advice they acquired an enormous collection of 19th century French art as well as works by artists such as Goya, El Greco and Titian.*

Much of the work that Cassatt produced between 1900–1922 was competent but lacked the freshness of vision and creative spark which had distinguished her earlier œuvre. Her paintings and pastels were more often than not of sweet-faced young girls, such as *Young Girl Reading* (see p. 87) or her *Sketch of Ellen Mary Cassatt* (see p. 88). There is no one explanation as to why she allowed her previously high standards to lapse. Very likely she was exhausted from the emotional strain of having lost her sister and parents within a span of less than twenty years. She and Degas saw little of each other, and she was kept busy with her work on behalf of the Havemeyers.

During much of her career Cassatt was what we would refer to today as an «artist's artist». With a few exceptions she was not given a great deal of attention in critical reviews and her sense of propriety kept her from the public eye. This is not to say that she was not pleased and flattered by recognition, simply that she did not actively seek it.

In 1904 her growing reputation began to manifest itself in the form of various honors and awards, including, at long last, recognition from her «compatriots.» The Pennsylvania Academy awarded her the Lippincott Prize of $300 at its 73rd annual exhibition for her painting entitled *Caress* (National Collection of Fine Arts, Smithsonian Institution). True to her principles Cassatt politely declined the award, reminding the members of the Academy

---

* Many of these paintings were subsequently donated to the Metropolitan Museum and other public collections.

THE BANJO LESSON, 1894. Pastel on paper, 28″ × 22½″ (71 × 57.2 cm)
Virginia Museum of Fine Arts, Richmond, Virginia

The Banjo Lesson, 1894. Drypoint and aquatint, II state, 11⅝″ × 9⅜″ (29.5 × 23.8 cm)
Minneapolis Institute of Arts. The Ladd Collection, Gift of Herschel V. Jones

PORTRAIT OF A WOMAN WITH A FAN, 1895. Pastel on paper, 26″ × 20″ (66 × 51 cm)
Collection: Mrs. Ellen M. Schuppli, Avon, Connecticut

THE PENSIVE READER, c. 1894. Pastel on paper, 20⅝″ × 17¼″ (52.5 × 43.8 cm)
Collection: Mr. and Mrs. Joseph H. Hirshhorn, Washington, D.C.

of the pledge she took when she joined the Independents: «no jury, no medals, no awards.»

One honor she happily accepted, however, was the *Légion d'honneur*, which was conferred upon her by the French government late in 1904.

As Cassatt entered her 60's she remained active and alert despite the toll that the passing years were taking on her, her family and friends. In December, 1906, her brother Alexander died, and one year later she was stunned to receive a cable from Louisine Havemeyer informing her of Mr. Havemeyer's death.

Only her brother Gardner remained from her immediate family, and in the fall of 1908 she made her last visit to the United States to visit him and his family. While they were together they made plans for an extensive trip across central Europe and through the eastern Mediterranean.

Two years later Gardner Cassatt and his family joined her in France and they set off on their trip. Despite her aversion to voyages by water, Cassatt agreed to climax their itinerary with a sail up the Nile in an Egyptian *dahabeah*. The trip ended in tragedy, however, as Gardner Cassatt became gravely ill and was rushed back to Paris. He died there on April 5, 1911.

Her brother's death precipitated a nervous breakdown for Cassatt, and her own ill health gradually prevented her from seeking solace in work, as she had so often done before. In 1912 she began to develop cataracts on her eyes, a condition that worsened as the years passed.

The work of her later years, such as *The Crochet Lesson* (see p. 86), was characterized by a deterioration in the draftsmanship which had once been her hallmark. Her pastels were executed with broad, slashing strokes and the colors assumed a greater and greater degree of stridency.

One cheering note during this period was the news that her *alma mater*, the Pennsylvania Academy of Art, had awarded her a Gold Medal of Honor. As the award was in recognition of her contributions to art rather than a «prize,» Cassatt accepted.

With the onset of World War I Cassatt was forced to evacuate Château Beaufresne (which was in the war zone) for the relative safety of Grasse. Even more upsetting to her was the forced separation from Mathilde Vallet, the faithful housekeeper upon whom she greatly relied.

Shortly before the end of the war she attended Degas' funeral, and subsequently wrote a description to Louisine Havemeyer:

> «Of course you have seen that Degas is no more. We buried
> him on Saturday, a beautiful sunshine, a little crowd of friends and
> admirers, all very quiet and peaceful in the midst of this dreadful
> upheaval of which he was barely conscious. You can well understand
> what a satisfaction it was to me to know that he had been well cared
> for and even tenderly nursed by his niece in his last days...»*

At the end of the war Cassatt was able to return to Château Beaufresne and was reunited with Mathilde. Her final years were lonely ones. She became an expatriate in time

---

* Cassatt herself had made these arrangements when she had heard that Degas was ill and alone.

IN THE GARDEN, 1893. Pastel on paper, 28¾" × 25⅝" (73 × 65 cm)
Baltimore Museum of Art. The Cone Collection

YOUNG MOTHER SEWING, 1902. Oil on canvas, 36¾″ × 29″ (92.3 × 73.7 cm)
The Metropolitan Museum of Art, New York. Bequest of Mrs. H. O. Havemeyer

LITTLE ANN SUCKING HER FINGER, EMBRACED BY HER MOTHER, 1897
Pastel on beige paper, 21¾″ × 17″ (55.3 × 43.2 cm). Jeu de Paume Museum, Paris

THE CROCHET LESSON, 1913. Pastel on paper, 30⅛″ × 25½″ (76.5 × 64.7 cm)
Private Collection

YOUNG GIRL READING, c. 1900–1910. Pastel on oatmeal paper mounted on linen, 25⅝″ × 19¾″ (65 × 50 cm)
Seattle Art Museum

SKETCH OF «ELLEN MARY CASSATT IN A BIG BLUE HAT», c. 1905. Oil on canvas, 24″ × 22″ (61 × 56 cm)
Collection: Mrs. Percy C. Madeira Jr., Berwyn, Pennsylvania

and space, overtaken by a world for which she little cared and which she little understood; she lapsed into a routine in which one day was virtually indistinguishable from the next.

Cassatt especially enjoyed her daily outing in the Renault landaulet which she had owned since 1906, insisting that it be kept in perfect working order. «We were not allowed a breakdown,» recalled her chauffeur, Armand Delaporte, in a letter to Cassatt's biographer Frederick Sweet. Despite her blindness she was so keenly aware of direction that she severely reprimanded Delaporte one day for changing their accustomed route to St. Cloud.

Her infrequent visitors, at least those who had known her in better times, were shocked at the thin, garrulous old woman who greeted them when they came to call. One such visitor was Forbes Watson, who found Cassatt:

> «...blind and lonely, unreasonable and vituperative, still a burning force and a dominant personality, capable of a violent burst of profanity in one breath and, with the next, of launching into a plea to save the coming generation of American art students from turning into café loafers in Paris...
>
> «"When I was young it was different," she appealed in a harrowing tone, touched with regret and apology, "Our museums had no great paintings for the students to study. Now that has been corrected* and something must be done to save our young American artists from wasting themselves over there." She waved her stick vaguely in the direction of the left bank.»**

George Biddle, who first made Cassatt's acquaintance while a young art student in Paris, wrote fondly of her shortly after her death:

> «If it is possible to love a purely detached enthusiasm, then I loved this prim old Philadelphia lady. How slim and upright she would sit in her white serge jacket and lace cap, her shawl sometimes spread over her knee, as she poured tea in the apartment in the Rue de Marignan — the wheezy, chocolate-eyed griffons subsiding in a coma of indigestion about her chair. And then as she caught on fire with some idea, her eyes blazed and narrowed, her capable bony hands jerked hither and thither... As the time to depart approached I would retreat step by step to the door...»***

Mary Stevenson Cassatt died at Château Beaufresne on June 14, 1926. Although it rained on the day of her funeral there was a large turnout by the local citizenry, including a band from a nearby village. Only a few of those present to honor her remembered Cassatt

---

* Cassatt was no doubt alluding to her own role in pushing for great public collections of art in the United States.
** *Mary Cassatt*, Whitney Museum, New York 1932.
*** *The Arts*, vol. 10, July-December 1926.

as anything more than the generous but aristocratic old woman who took her daily drive in the familiar Renault landaulet. A handful of her old friends were able to reach the area in time for the funeral, one of them Ambroise Vollard, who wrote:

« In the cemetery, after the last prayers, the pastor, according to Protestant custom, distributed to those present the roses and carnations strewn upon the coffin, that they might scatter them over the grave. Looking at this carpet of beautiful flowers, I fancied Mary Cassatt running to fetch a canvas and brushes. »

No doubt she would have been pleased at that idea.

JAY ROUDEBUSH

PORTRAIT OF MADAME A. F. AUDE AND HER TWO DAUGHTERS, 1899
Pastel on grey paper, 21⅜" × 31⅞" (54.3 × 81 cm). Private collection, Paris

BIOGRAPHY

1844 Born May 22, in Allegheny City, Pennsylvania, fourth surviving child of Mr. and Mrs. Robert Simpson Cassatt.

1851 Family moves to Europe, settling in Paris. They remain in Paris two years.

1853–1855 Family moves to Heidelberg and Darmstadt. Brother Robbie dies and family returns to America.

1861–1865 Enrolled as a student at the Pennsylvania Academy of Fine Arts.

1866 To Paris, enrolling briefly in atelier of Charles Chaplin.

1868 First Salon acceptance with *The Mandolin Player*.

1870 Forced to return to Philadelphia by outbreak of Franco-Prussian war.

1871 To Parma, Italy, to study paintings of Correggio and Parmigianino. Also studies printmaking with Carlo Raimondi at local academy.

1872 Second Salon acceptance with *Pendant le Carnaval*.

1873 Travels to Madrid, Seville, Belgium and the Netherlands, studying Spanish, Flemish and Dutch masters. Third Salon acceptance with *Torero and Young Girl*. Settles permanently in Paris, where she meets Louisine Waldron Elder (later Mrs. Henry O. Havemeyer).

1874 First exhibition of the Impressionists. *Portrait of Madame Cortier* accepted by Salon and praised by Degas.

1877 Meets Degas and is invited to join the Impressionists. Parents and sister Lydia arrive in Paris to settle permanently.

1879 Participates in fourth Impressionist exhibition. Works with Pissarro and Degas on journal of original prints, to be called «Le Jour et La Nuit.»

1880 Participates in fifth Impressionist exhibition. Brother Alexander Cassatt and family pay extended visit.

1881 Participates in sixth Impressionist exhibition.

1882 Her sister, Lydia, dies. Joins Degas in refusing to participate in seventh Impressionist exhibition.

1886 Participates in eighth — and last — Impressionist exhibit. Duurand-Ruel organizes Impressionist show in New York.

1890 With Degas visits great exhibition of Japanese prints at Ecole des Beaux-Arts. Begins work on a series of ten color prints.

1891 First individual show at Durand-Ruel's, Paris, featuring ten color prints, two oils and two pastels. Father, Robert Simpson Cassatt, dies.

1892 Begins work on mural for Chicago World's Fair. Purchases Château Beaufresne, at Mesnil-Théribus, Oise.

1893 Major individual show at Durand-Ruel's, Paris, consisting of 98 works.

1895 Major individual show at Durand-Ruel's gallery in New York. Mother, Mrs. Robert Simpson Cassatt, dies.

1898 First visit to United States since 1870.

1901 Extended trip through Italy and Spain with Mr. and Mrs. H. O. Havemeyer, advising them on purchase of paintings.

1904 Made a *Chevalier de la Légion d'honneur* by the French government.

1906 Death of her brother, Alexander Cassatt.

1908 Last visit to United States.

1911–1912 Extended trip through Europe and Middle East with brother Gardner and family. Gardner dies after becoming ill in Egypt. Suffers nervous breakdown.

1914 Individual show at Durand-Ruel's, Paris. Awarded Gold Medal of Honor by Pennsylvania Academy. Stops work due to blindness.

1914–1918 Forced to evacuate Château Beaufresne during World War I. Degas dies in 1917.

1926 Dies at Château Beaufresne, June 14.

We wish to thank Mrs. Adelyn Breeskin, the owners of the pictures by Mary Cassatt reproduced in this book, as well as those collectors who did not wish to have their names mentioned:

MUSEUMS

FRANCE
Bibliothèque Nationale, Paris – Louvre Museum, Paris – Museum of the Petit-Palais, Paris.

UNITED KINGDOM
Glasgow Art Gallery.

U.S.A.
Baltimore Museum of Art – The Museum of Fine Arts, Boston – The Art Institute of Chicago – The Flint Museum of Arts, Michigan – The Nelson Atkins Museum, Kansas City – The Los Angeles County Museum of Art – The Norton Simon Foundation, Los Angeles – The Metropolitan Museum of Art, New York – The Minneapolis Institute of Arts – The New Britain Museum of American Art, Connecticut – The Chrysler Museum at Norfolk, Virginia – The Philadelphia Museum of Art – Museum of Art, Carnegie Institute, Pittsburgh – The Virginia Museum of Fine Arts, Richmond, Virginia – The Seattle Art Museum – St. Louis Art Museum – The Corcoran Gallery of Art, Washington, D.C. – The National Gallery of Art, Washington, D.C. – National Portrait Gallery, Smithsonian Institution, Washington, D.C. – The Wichita Art Museum, Kansas – The Sterling and Francine Clark Art Institute, Williamstown, Massachusetts – The Worcester Art Museum, Massachusetts.

PRIVATE COLLECTIONS

Mrs. Adelyn D. Breeskin, Washington, D.C. – F. G. Bührle Foundation, Zurich – Nathan Cummings, New York – Mr. and Mrs. Joseph H. Hirshhorn, Washington, D.C. – Mrs. Percy C. Madeira Jr., Berwyn, Pennsylvania – Mr. and Mrs. Paul Mellon, Upperville, Virginia – Everett D. Reese, Columbus, Ohio   Mrs. Ellen M. Schuppli, Avon, Connecticut – The Virginia Steele Scott Foundation, Pasadena, California.

PHOTOGRAPHS

E. Irving Blomstrann, New Britain, Conn. – Will Brown, Philadelphia – Bulloz, Paris – Walter Dräyer, Zurich – Studio Lourmel, Paris – Otto E. Nelson, New York – Eric Pollitzer, New York – Service de Documentation Photographique de la Réunion des Musées Nationaux, Paris – Elton Schnellbacher, Pittsburgh – John Tennant, Mt. Airy, Maryland – Frank J. Thomas, Los Angeles – A. J. Wyatt, Philadelphia.